Telemarketing Tips from A to Z

How to Make Every Call a Winner!

Nancy Friedman

The Telephone Doctor®

A Fifty-Minute™ Series Book

This Fifty-Minute™ book is designed to be "read with a pencil." It is an excellent workbook for self-study as well as classroom learning. All material is copyright-protected and cannot be duplicated without permission from the publisher. *Therefore, be sure to order a copy for every training participant by contacting:*

CRISP. Learning
Menlo Park, California

1-800-442-7477

CrispLearning.com

Telemarketing Tips from A to Z

How to Make Every Call a Winner!

Nancy Friedman

CREDITS:
Senior Editor: **Debbie Woodbury**
Copy Editor: **Charlotte Bosarge**
Production Manager: **Judy Petry**
Design: **Amy Shayne**
Production Artist: **Zach Hooker, Darin Stumme**
Cartoonist: **Ralph Mapson**

© 2001 Crisp Publications, Inc.
Printed in the United States of America by Von Hoffmann Graphics, Inc.

CrispLearning.com

01 02 03 04   10 9 8 7 6 5 4 3 2 1

Library of Congress Catalog Card Number 00-110384
Friedman, Nancy
Telemarketing Tips from A to Z
ISBN 1-56052-603-3

Learning Objectives For:

TELEMARKETING TIPS FROM A TO Z

The objectives for *Telemarketing Tips from A to Z* are listed below.
They have been developed to guide you, the reader, to the core issues
covered in this book.

THE OBJECTIVES OF THIS BOOK ARE:

❑ 1) To present skills and techniques involved in effective
       telemarketing

❑ 2) To show how to gain more from every call, both outgoing
       and incoming

❑ 3) To indicate mistakes common to telemarketing and suggest how to
       avoid making them

ASSESSING YOUR PROGRESS

In addition to the learning objectives, Crisp Learning has developed an
assessment that covers the fundamental information presented in this
book. A 25 item, multiple-choice/true-false questionnaire allows the reader
to evaluate his or her comprehension of the subject matter. To learn how
to obtain a copy of this assessment please call: **1-800-442-7477** and ask to
speak with a Customer Service Representative.

Assessments should not be used in any selection process.

How to Use This Book

This *Fifty-Minute™ Series Book* is a unique, user-friendly product. As you read through the material, you will quickly experience the interactive nature of the book. There are numerous exercises, real-world case studies, and examples that invite your opinion, as well as checklists, tips, and concise summaries that reinforce your understanding of the concepts presented.

A Crisp Learning *Fifty-Minute™ Book* can be used in variety of ways. Individual self-study is one of the most common. However, many organizations use *Fifty-Minute* books for pre-study before a classroom training session. Other organizations use the books as a part of a system-wide learning program—supported by video and other media based on the content in the books. Still others work with Crisp Learning to customize the material to meet their specific needs and reflect their culture. Regardless of how it is used, we hope you will join the more than 20 million satisfied learners worldwide who have completed a *Fifty-Minute Book*.

Preface

Successful telemarketing is largely common sense, using basic skills and techniques. It's not brain surgery or rocket science. It involves trying to be thoughtful and focused when calling out or taking incoming calls. Let's not make it more difficult than it is.

To get the most from this book, we recommend you underline or highlight those ideas that you want to use.

We've taken what we feel are the most important basic telemarketing tips, skills, and techniques and put them in the book. In the future, electronic technology will change, but the all-important "people skills"–the suggestions in this book– are timeless. They will never go out of style!

So, enjoy and profit...and remember the Telephone Doctor® motto:

"IT'S FUN TO BE GOOD!"

Nancy

Nancy Friedman
The Telephone Doctor®

Dedication _____

This book is dedicated to anyone who has ever used a telephone in a business setting to make outgoing calls, take incoming calls, sell to new customers, or serve existing customers.

Your efforts on the telephone contribute substantially to the success of your organization. Those of us involved in telephone sales and service sincerely appreciate your efforts. This is, therefore, a book dedicated to YOU.

About the Author

Nancy Friedman, the Telephone Doctor®, has been bringing telephone and customer service skills to thousands of organizations in the United States and abroad for 15 years. The Telephone Doctor® library includes 16 video-based teaching programs on customer service, and is available in seven languages in 27 countries. Nancy is also the author of *Telephone Skills from A to Z* and *Customer Service Nightmares,* both available from Crisp Learning.

The Telephone Doctor® is regarded as the "foremost and most sought-after speaker on telephone skills and customer service."

Nancy can be reached at:

Telephone Doctor®
30 Hollenberg Ct.
St. Louis, MO 63044
314-291-1012
Fax: 314-291-3710
email: Nancy@telephonedoctor.com
Website: www.telephonedoctor.com

Thank You —————————————————

Thank you to Jeanne Fitzler, of Telephone Doctor® who helped compile this information. Her patience is a vitrue.

Thanks too, to all the Telephone Doctor® staff, who walk our walk…and talk our talk. We know it works.

To my husband Dick, who's always there for me…and to my children, David, Linda, and their spouses, Robyn and Les…thank you for all your support.

Contents

x

Introduction

✔ **Fact:** The word *telemarketing* is defined in the *American Heritage College Dictionary* as, "(Noun) Use of the telephone in marketing."

✔ **Fact:** The word *telemarketer* is NOT in the *American Heritage College Dictionary.*

✔ **Fact:** The word *telemarketing* is indeed a well-known and often-used word. (Some swearing by it, and some swearing at it.)

✔ **Fact:** There are tools you can use to become a more effective telemarketer.

✔ **Fact:** This book is one of them.

✔ **Fact:** Telemarketing is a full-fledged, respectable, money-making industry.

There are two types of telemarketing calls:

➤ **Outbound**

➤ **Inbound**

The Outbound Telemarketer

Have you ever been sitting down to dinner with your favorite person over a beautiful candlelit table, the phone rings and you hear, "Hi, Mr. Smith. How are you tonight?" That is the outbound telemarketing call. Usually it is business-to-consumer. Outbound calls are the calls you receive trying to get you to buy or register for something. They can be frustrating, annoying, and almost always an interruption. Most likely, the telemarketer has not been trained effectively on how to make a phone call that won't annoy and frustrate you.

There are also outbound business-to-business calls. Those are the calls made to businesses trying to capture your attention to purchase something. For example, a copy machine sales rep calling a company to try and get their business or sell a machine is a business-to-business call.

The Inbound Telemarketer

The other side of the coin is the inbound telemarketer. These are the folks that take call after call from a central location—answering questions, taking orders, handling complaints, and filling in forms. Most of these people are employed in call centers. Rather than selling something, these telemarketers may be taking information or answering questions from someone who has called them. They may also try to *up-sell* or *cross-sell*.

Whether you work outbound or inbound, this book is for you. You will find tips and techniques to make you more efficient and more effective on the telephone. These Telephone Doctor® skills are tried, true, tested, and best of all—*they work*!

Attitude: It's Your Choice

You have little or no control over many things in life. However, you do have control over one essential factor: Your attitude.

Disinterested, bored, unmotivated people are not very productive, and they achieve little satisfaction in life. In contrast, people who make an effort to have a positive and cheerful attitude typically reach many of their goals and usually are happier and more fulfilled!

Successful people normally have already made decisions about their attitude. They get to know enough about themselves to understand how to control their attitude.

Consider this example: You are driving your car in rush-hour traffic. A car swerves in front of you without signaling and cuts you off. You can get mad and swear at the other driver, or you can stay "cool"—it is *your choice*. If you get upset, you give control of your attitude to the other driver. If you stay calm, you control your attitude!

Remember: No one else can affect your attitude unless you let them.

It is the same way at work and in life. Once you've figured this out, you will stay positive whether you are dealing with a mean, nasty person or the nicest person in the world!

You can control your attitude. No one can affect you unless you let them. So when you open your eyes in the morning and get out of bed, you need to understand that you have a choice. What kind of attitude will you decide to have that day? It's up to you. Don't let anyone else control the way you act!

If your job consists of making or taking phone calls—if you are in the lucrative telemarketing industry—your attitude is going to make all the difference in the success of your career. Make it a great one!

1. Regardless of circumstances, you always control your own attitude.

2. Your attitude can improve the worst situation, or ruin the best one.

3. Successful people consciously choose a positive attitude.

ATTITUDE: IT'S YOUR CHOICE

There are many things in life (like the weather, rush-hour traffic and restaurant ketchup bottles) that you simply can't control. What is the one thing you do control that can help to compensate for others?

_____

_____

Isn't a positive attitude one of those qualities that a person either has or doesn't have? If not, how do you get one? What specific characteristics can you develop to make your attitude more positive?

_____

_____

List three things that frustrate you, how you react to those frustrations, and then how you feel you could control them by your attitude.

What frustrates me?	How do I react?	How can I control my frustration better with my attitude?

Example:

I get frustrated by rush-hour traffic.	I swear a lot.	I can control my attitude by realizing that swearing isn't going to help. In fact, if the person in the other car heard me, it would do more damage.

1. _____ _____ _____
   _____ _____ _____
   _____
   _____

2. _____ _____ _____
   _____ _____ _____
   _____
   _____

3. _____ _____ _____
   _____ _____ _____
   _____
   _____

 Benefits

There are benefits and there are features. Maybe you think they are the same thing. Well, they're not.

What is the difference between benefits and features? Here are the definitions:

Feature:

1.   A distinction or noticeable quality

2.   Something offered as a special attraction

Benefits:

1.   Anything that is helpful or advantageous

2.   Something that contributes to, or increases, well-being

Consider the difference. Let's say a manufacturer introduces a new car with an oversized fuel tank. The fuel tank would be the *feature*.

What would the benefit be? Well, with an oversized fuel tank, the driver wouldn't have to go to the gas station as often. One could drive for hundreds of miles on one tank of gas, saving time and effort. That would be a *benefit*.

The reason we're talking about features and benefits is because benefits are what the customer buys. You'll be a more effective telemarketer if you can answer the question every customer asks, "What's In It For Me?" (The old radio station WIIFM.)

After you mention a *feature*, use the magic words, "What that means to you is..." Then describe the *benefits*.

Example:

> *"Our bank has just installed a new automatic teller machine in your neighborhood, Mr. Jones (feature), and WHAT THAT MEANS TO YOU is now you can get cash conveniently 24 hours a day, seven days a week (benefit)."*

When you are on the phone trying to sell a product or a service, especially to someone you have never met and probably never will, it is very important to remember that features and benefits are what they want to hear. They want to hear what you have to offer and how that product or service will benefit them.

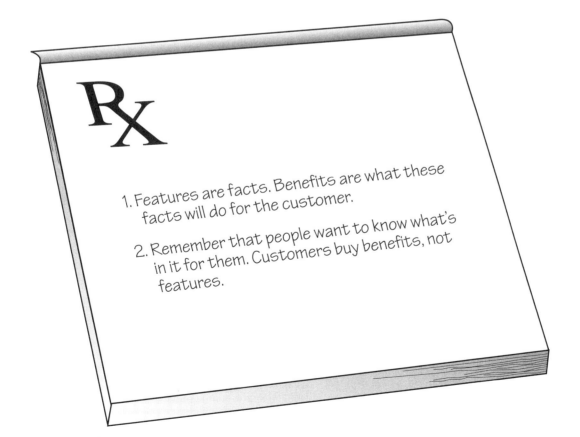

Rx

1. Features are facts. Benefits are what these facts will do for the customer.

2. Remember that people want to know what's in it for them. Customers buy benefits, not features.

BENEFITS

Your organization's products and services have features or characteristics that make them unique. What converts these features into benefits for your customer and sales for your organization?

_____

_____

What phrase will make it easier to discuss benefits with your customers?

_____

_____

List three features of one of your products or services. Then, after the words "What this means to you is..." write the benefits.

Feature		Benefits
1.		
2.	"What this means to you is…"	
3.		

Closing Techniques

Entire books have been written on the subject of closing the sale. *Closing* is the method of getting the customer to agree to purchase what is being offered. There are literally dozens of closing techniques. These can be words, offerings, incentives, and so on. Most people need a reason to buy what you're offering. Simply telling them about something and having them take it isn't selling—it's luck.

Let's take a closer look:

Closing is the question or series of questions you ask, or the action you take, that results in a commitment to do business. Closing questions are very common and very gentle.

The two types of closing questions are:

➤ **Single Closing Questions**

➤ **Dual Closing Questions**

Single Closing Questions

The single closing question allows the prospect (your customer) to answer a question that results in getting the order.

Example:

You have just offered your prospect or client a new magazine that comes out eight times a year. You could ask a single closing question as follows:

> *"Would you like to go ahead with this subscription?"*
>
> *"When would you want to receive your order?"*
>
> *"Where should we mail the first copy?"*

Any one of these three would be a good *closing* question.

Dual Closing Questions

Dual closing questions have also been called *alternative of choice*. Using dual closing questions are a useful tool to learn. Basically, you offer your customer two choices—either answer confirms your sale.

Example:

> *"Will you need one or two subscriptions?"*
>
> *"Would you prefer delivery on Friday or would Monday be better?"*
>
> *"Do you prefer monthly payments, or would an annual payment be more convenient?"*

Dual closing questions give the customer two "goodies" to choose from.

True Tales

Here's a true story about my son, David. When David was young he didn't want to eat his vegetables. Like any concerned mother, I felt that asking him every night would do the trick. "David, do you want vegetables?" Every night, the same question and the same answer: "No thanks." And so on it went, until I got smart. One night I asked him, "David, do you want corn or peas?" His answer—without missing a beat—was "Corn!" You see, I gave him a dual question.

Two things—either answer would have made me happy. He had his vegetables. It works!

A major reason most business is lost is simply that the rep doesn't ask the prospect to buy. It's that simple: Without asking for the business, you're just having a conversation.

Most closing questions are usually asked near the end of the conversation, although there are times when you may ask closing questions midway through the conversation.

When closing, remember to use what Telephone Doctor® calls *buffers* before your single or dual closing questions. Buffers are the words used prior to the closing question. Buffers soften the process.

Example:

> *"Let me ask you a question: When would you like me to ship your order?"*

"Let me ask you a question..." are the buffer words.

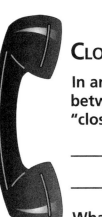

CLOSING

In any customer contact, the closing is what makes the difference between a conversation and a transaction. What exactly does "closing a sale" mean?

_____

_____

What are the essential elements of a close?

_____

_____

Write a single closing question.

_____

_____

Write a dual closing question.

_____

_____

1. A major reason business is lost is that no one ever asked the prospect to buy.

2. Without a close, a customer contact is only a conversation, not a transaction.

3. Be sure to ask closing questions.

Details

Here's a phone message form...what is missing?

PHONE CALL

FOR _____ *Judy* _____ DATE _____ TIME _____ A.M. P.M.	
M _____ *John*	
OF _____ *John & Co.*	✔ PHONED
PHONE _____ ☐ FAX ☐ MOBILE	RETURNED YOUR CALL
AREA CODE NUMBER EXTENSION	✔ PLEASE CALL
MESSAGE _____	WILL CALL AGAIN
_____	CAME TO SEE YOU
_____	WANTS TO SEE YOU
SIGNED ▼Tops FORM 4003	

Where is the phone number? The person receiving the message may know more than one John. Which John? What time did he call? Was it today? Who took the message? You need to find that person and try to get more information!

Improper message-taking is costing businesses hundreds of thousands of dollars a year. This is money leaking through the phone wires due to poorly taken messages.

True, not all callers will volunteer the information you need. So, if the caller doesn't offer his or her name, phone number, etc., use Telephone Doctor®'s "AND..." technique to get the caller to fill in the blanks. It seldom fails.

> "*Yes, Mrs. Smith. AND your phone number is....*"

> "*AND your company is....*"

All the caller needs to do is fill in the blanks. It is easy and very, very effective.

Little Details Can Cause Big Mistakes

The little detail of a time and date can cost your company big time. And frankly, messages without a date and time are useless. The date and time are critical to every message. These types of details can prevent mistakes and save time. The few extra seconds it may take to acquire these details could save hours later, to say nothing of saving an order. They might even keep a company from losing a customer. They are the little things that count and must be done!

Details are also useful for unisex names. Have you ever taken a message from a Pat, Chris, Lee, or another unisex name? They need to have the Mr. or Ms. in front of the name. A small detail, but very important. After all, only the person taking the message can hear the caller's voice and (usually) tell if the customer is male or female.

What about those people whose voices make it difficult to determine gender? I find that if you can get the person to laugh, you usually can tell the difference. Women seem to laugh more in an upper register, while men tend to laugh in the lower register. It's not foolproof, but it's better than not trying or not knowing.

Back to details. Every industry has various and important details that if missed, can create havoc, and make business more difficult than necessary.

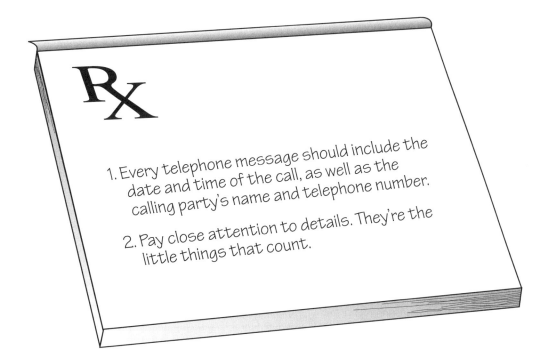

R_X

1. Every telephone message should include the date and time of the call, as well as the calling party's name and telephone number.

2. Pay close attention to details. They're the little things that count.

14

DETAILS

The only thing worse than not getting a telephone message is getting one that is incomplete. What details must be included in each telephone message that you take?

_____

_____

Come up with some of the details that are important in your particular business, and make a list of what can happen if those details are missed.

1. _____

_____

2. _____

_____

3. _____

_____

How can you be sure these details are attended to each time? (What can you personally do to assure that the details are not missed?)

1. _____

_____

2. _____

_____

3. _____

_____

*E*cho Questions

Every once in a while, you will need additional information or clarification from the person you're talking with, or maybe you need something repeated.

Phrases such as "What?" "Huh?" or "What did you say?" can sound threatening or disrespectful.

There is a much more effective technique called the "echo question." It has also been referred to as mirroring, reflecting, or parroting.

To use an echo question, you begin your sentence with the last few words the other person has just said to you. Then convert that statement into a question by slightly raising your voice at the end. Pause for more information from the person.

Example:

> **Caller:** *"Go ahead and ship the order. I need it tomorrow for a meeting."*
>
> **You:** *"For a meeting?"*
>
> **Caller:** *"Yes. I am meeting with the new production manager, Jim Jones, and he wants to get going on this project. And by the way, please put Mr. Jones in your computer database so he will get mail from you also."*

See how much more information you got from just one echo question? And the clarification was non-confrontational.

Another example:

Caller: *"There are some problems with the policy your company just sent me."*

You: *"Problems with the policy we just sent you?"*

Caller: *"Yes, the policy doesn't say anything about covering our little storage building, and I definitely wanted that listed."*

If your instinct is to say "What problem?" that's pretty average, and it is okay if you want to *remain* average. However, by asking the echo question you will get far more information. This technique enables you to get additional information in a much smoother way.

Rx

1. Use echo questions to get more information in a very smooth way.

2. Phrase your question using the key words from the caller's last statement.

3. Raise the tone of your voice slightly at the end to make the words a question.

ECHO

Echo questions, using the customer's last few words to form an inquiry, are a smooth and effective way of gathering more information. What are some advantages of using this technique?

_____

_____

What are three things you should do when asking an echo question?

1. _____

2. _____

3. _____

List three statements that a customer might say to you, and write your echo question beneath each.

1. Caller: _____

   Echo Question: _____

_____

2. Caller: _____

   Echo Question: _____

_____

3. Caller: _____

   Echo Question: _____

_____

DEF 3 Finish the Day Ready to Begin

This almost sounds like, "Up the street the soldiers are marching down," doesn't it? This particular technique is an important one if you want to learn to be more productive.

Answer this question as honestly as you can:

When you get ready to go home at night, what does your work area look like?

_____

_____

Remember that what you leave at night will be waiting for you the next morning when you come to work. "Be Prepared" is more than the Boy Scout motto, it is a way of life for a professional.

Before you leave work for the day, organize your work area for the next day. Have a list of calls ready for when you get back to your desk. Put a few calls you are excited to make at the top of the list. You will make those first and, if you're excited, the calls will start off in a more positive manner.

It is much easier and healthier to work in an area that is neat and inviting rather than messy. It also helps to have a list of your top-priority projects ready so you can start the day off right.

If you are the type who has a messy desk and yet defends this with, "It may be messy, but at least I know where everything is," you are still losing valuable time because of the work habits and methods you use. Take a few extra minutes at the end of the day to straighten up your area. It can add dollars to your phone calls.

FINISH THE DAY READY TO BEGIN

Finishing each day ready to start the next one sounds simple, but it's a process that has definite steps and definite benefits. Take a few moments to list some of the specific things you can do to prepare your work area for the next day and note at least one positive result of each one.

If I take time today to…	Then, tomorrow…
1.	
2.	
3.	

How did your work area look this morning? What changes can you make the next time you leave to prepare it better for your return?

_____

_____

℞

1. Finish the day ready to begin.

2. Remember, what you leave today will be waiting for you when you return.

Greetings

If you knew a particular food made you sick, you would probably avoid it, wouldn't you?

And if you knew that a certain intersection was dangerous and there were lots of accidents and delays there, you would go another way, wouldn't you?

Now, what if you knew a particular phone greeting was a "killer phrase?" You'd stop using it, wouldn't you?

Well, here is one greeting that can kill the start of any phone conversation:

> *"Hi. How are you?"*

Ask that question and you might get a response like:

> *"Oh, I'm so glad you asked. My arthritis is acting up; my back is just killing me; I have a migraine that won't quit; my pacemaker's running a little slow and the corns on my toes are hurting like mad. How are you?"*

The words "How are you?" to a person you have never met or spoken to before–and may never again–can be a killer greeting. It is not only important that you stop using them, you should also understand why they should be avoided.

You might be saying to yourself: "My goodness! 'How are you?' It's harmless! I use it all the time." True, it is harmless in *certain* conversations such as those with someone you know or have spoken to before. But on the telephone, with someone you are speaking to for the first time, it can be very dangerous.

Why using "How are you?" is risky:

1. You probably don't really care how they are, so it is insincere (and your caller will know it).

2. You are giving up control of the conversation.

3. "How are you?" is usually regarded as a tip-off that you are trying to sell something.

Instead of "How are you," learn to use other socially acceptable phrases that are friendly, but don't give control of the conversation to the other person.

A few Telephone Doctor® examples of acceptable phrases are:

"Hello, Mr. Smith, nice to meet you by phone."

"Hi, Mary, I'm glad we can spend a few moments together. The reason I'm calling...."

"Good afternoon, Mr. Jones. I appreciate you having a few minutes for me."

Remember: Avoid the killer phrases "How are you today?" and, "Hi, how are you?" These cliché phrases are simply not necessary on any call to someone you have not had prior contact with.

GREETINGS

The four killer words "How are you today?" have the power to kill a new conversation, a sales prospect, or even a good day. Why is this such a dangerous question, particularly with someone you're speaking to for the first time?

_____

_____

Recall a recent telephone call you received in which you were greeted with "How are you today?" If your reaction was negative, it probably changed the course of the conversation. How would a reaction like that from your customers make your job harder?

_____

_____

Make a list of alternative greetings for your work area to remind you that there are effective alternatives to the four killer words.

_____

_____

1. When greeting customers, avoid the four killer words: "How are you today?".

2. Use a creative alternative to begin the conversation.

*H*umor

Everyone likes to laugh, even customers and prospective customers.

Here is an example of a caller trying to enjoy a phone call and the rep not "getting it."

Caller: (Playfully)   *"I'm calling to place an order for more checks, because you're the world's greatest bank!"*

Rep: (Grimly)   *"Okay, what's your account number?"*

Talk about dropping the ball. When a caller is in a good mood or sharing a little humor, it is okay to play along. In fact, if you don't, the caller can be offended. At the same time, don't go off the deep end and risk offending the caller.

It's not necessary to come back with:

Rep: *"Hey, have you heard the one about the traveling salesman and the farmer's daughter?"*

That's going too far! When the other party tries humor, it is more appropriate to respond in kind. Let's see how the rep should have responded.

Caller: *"I'm calling to order more checks, because you're the world's greatest bank!"*

Rep: *"Not only are you correct, madam, but you're obviously someone of great intelligence (BIG SMILE). May I have your account number, please?"*

In this way, you can use a little humor and it can go a long way. It humanizes the relationship. If someone you're talking to uses a little humor, build rapport by acknowledging it. Use some gentle humor back. Everyone likes to smile. Even—believe it or not—when there's a problem.

HUMOR

Humor can be a very effective tool in building rapport with customers. However, like any other tool, it can cause a lot of damage if used incorrectly. What precautions can you take to make sure you use this tool safely?

_____

_____

Think of some times where you could have used a little humor and missed the boat. This will help you in the future.

1. _____

2. _____

3. _____

List the negative effects of using too much humor or too little.

TOO MUCH HUMOR	TOO LITTLE HUMOR
1.	1.
2.	2.
3.	3.

1. When the other party uses humor, respond in kind with gentle humor.

2. Be careful to use humor appropriately.

"*I*" Irritates

Have you ever had irritated eyes? Perhaps you've gotten something in them.

Why are we talking about irritated eyes? Well, because it is important for you to remember the word "I" irritates. Everyone you talk with is interested in themselves. Remember radio station WIIFM? Not What's In It For You.

When your conversation is loaded with "I have," "I knew," or, "I should," it does not sound like you are focused on the customer.

Let's consider two ways of saying something:

> *"I want you to try this. I think it really has merit. I've got lots of satisfied customers. I can have you covered by Wednesday. I say let's go!"*

See how many times "I" was used? Here's a better way:

> *"Mr. Jones, please try this. You'll really enjoy it. It makes a lot of sense for you. We've had hundreds of satisfied customers who renew this plan again and again. Plus, you can have immediate coverage. Let's go ahead, okay?"*

One more thing: If you do need an authority figure, instead of using "I," consider using "The experts say," or "Our president recently said...". These are much more acceptable, and they build credibility.

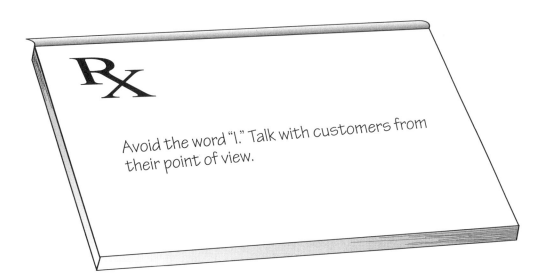

Avoid the word "I." Talk with customers from their point of view.

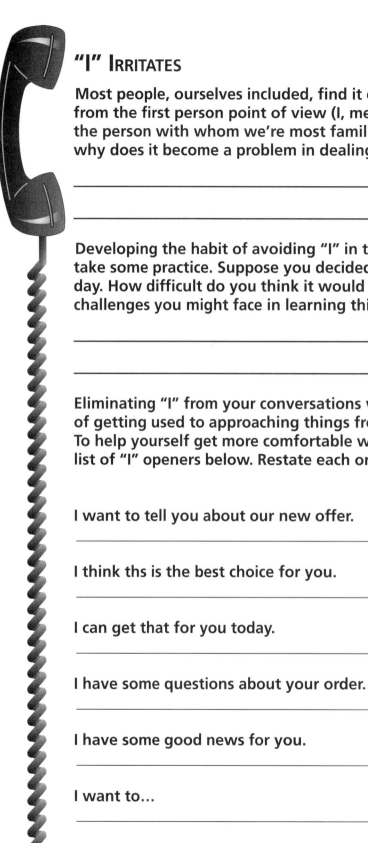

"I" IRRITATES

Most people, ourselves included, find it easiest to view things from the first person point of view (I, me, my, etc.). After all, that's the person with whom we're most familiar. If this is so natural, why does it become a problem in dealing with customers?

_____

_____

Developing the habit of avoiding "I" in talking with customers will take some practice. Suppose you decided to quit using "I" for one day. How difficult do you think it would be? List some of the challenges you might face in learning this skill.

_____

_____

Eliminating "I" from your conversations with customers is a matter of getting used to approaching things from a different direction. To help yourself get more comfortable with doing that, review the list of "I" openers below. Restate each one without "I."

I want to tell you about our new offer.

_____

I think ths is the best choice for you.

_____

I can get that for you today.

_____

I have some questions about your order.

_____

I have some good news for you.

_____

I want to…

_____

I think…

_____

Jerry's Pet Peeve

My late brother, Jerry, was a professional sales trainer. He really understood what helped people to buy, and also what killed or stopped a sale. One of his biggest pet peeves was talking yourself *out* of an order.

Example:

> **You:** *"Hi, Mr. Johnson, I'm Beth Jones from First Gigantic Bank."*
>
> **Client:** *"First Gigantic Bank? I recently had a bad experience with your bank."*
>
> **You:** *"Oh. So, then you probably wouldn't be interested in opening a new checking account with us, would you?"*
>
> **Client:** *"That's right!"*
>
> **You:** *"Well, okay. Thanks, good-bye."*

Be careful not to cement a negative when it is not necessary. Don't turn a prospect's objection into a suicide question that kills the conversation. Rather, ask what happened. Get more details. It could be a curable situation. Find out if you can help.

Example:

> **You:** *"Hi, Mr. Johnson, I'm Beth Jones from First Gigantic Bank."*
>
> **Client:** *"First Gigantic Bank? I recently had a bad experience with your bank."*
>
> **You:** *"My goodness. I'm sorry to hear that! Tell me what happened."*

Saying "okay" is not always okay

It is NOT okay to approve a negative. If I told you that you wouldn't be getting your paycheck this week, would you say "okay"? Of course not. You'd want to know why. You'd ask questions.

When you offer someone something and they don't take advantage of it and you simply say "okay," that makes you average. You don't want to be average, do you?

Stretch. Go for the excellence. Go for above average. Don't approve a negative.

JERRY'S PET PEEVE

When a customer raises an objection or makes a negative comment early in a sales contact, there is a tendency to accept the situation, abandon the contact, and move on to something more promising. Why would an otherwise effective sales person make such a mistake?

_____

_____

Providing excellent customer service means exceeding the needs of our customers. By making a negative comment or raising an instant objection, the customer seems to be telling us we have failed to do so. What should (and should not) be done in a situation like this?

_____

_____

Don't cement a negative or objection. Get details by asking questions.

Know Your Objective

How would you feel if on your next flight you heard the following announcement?

> *"Ladies and gentlemen, this is the captain speaking from the flight deck. We'll be taking off shortly. I have no idea what city we're going to. So, let's just get this bird in the air and we'll figure it out from there. Now sit back and enjoy your flight. Thanks for flying No-Objective Airlines."*

Not very comforting, is it? Is it any different when you're on the telephone? A common trait of successful telesales professionals is the ability to determine their call objectives before they've dialed the phone number.

A call objective is what you plan to achieve during a phone call. An objective can be as simple as getting a name or a certain bit of information, or as complicated as making a large sale.

Example:

> *"My objective here will be to find out the next time Mr. Green will be in the office."*

> *"At the end of this call I hope to have the name and phone number of the plant manager in Paducah."*

> *"If this call is successful, I'll be closing an order covering a health group of 1,500."*

Whatever your specific objective is, you'll feel more successful when you are reaching your objectives many times a day.

Be sure you know your objectives. Jot them down before you make the call. Know where you're going. When you hang up, be sure you reached at least one of your objectives.

KNOW YOUR OBJECTIVE

Why is it important for effective communication that we focus on such an apparently simple and obvious point as knowing your objective?

_____

_____

What is the relationship between objectives and success?

_____

_____

List three objectives you might need to achieve in your job when calling someone or taking a call.

1. _____

2. _____

3. _____

Be sure you know your objective before every call.

32

 # Let's

One of the biggest reasons people don't buy is that no one asks them to. Quite often, the buyer is on the fence, but the salesperson doesn't say anything. So the buyer, who is still unconvinced, says he wants to think about it. It happens everyday.

There is a word that *gently* asks people to buy. The word is *let's*.

Let's is the word used to show cooperation with the buyer. It is gentle, low pressure, and perfect! You gently urge prospects to go in the direction you'd like them to. For instance:

> *"Let's get all the information so we can ship when you're ready."*

> *"Let's talk about when you need this so you can take advantage of our special offer."*

Let's is a cooperative word that encourages the customer to do something, usually positive. It tells customers that you are with them and that they are not alone. Customers will feel as though you're on their team with the *Let's Technique*.

Think about teachers getting young kids to do what needs to be done in the classroom.

Teacher: *"Let's clean up our toys, and then we can go out to recess."*

By using this technique, the teacher is telling the class, "I'm here with you..." and the children respond in a very positive manner. So will your customers.

Let's is a momentum word. It starts motion and movement where there was none before. Will it work all the time? Probably not. Will it work most of the time? Absolutely!

Rx

1. "Let's" shows cooperation with buyers. It's low-pressure and perfect.

2. "Let's" maintains control of the conversation.

3. "Let's" displays confidence in your ability and customers will comply.

LET'S

"Let's" makes a smooth transition from the information portion of your contact to the decision part, but it can also influence the customer's decision to buy. How can that be?

____

____

Rewrite the following statements using "let's." Let's go!

"Give me your shipping address so I can process your order."

____

____

"Do you have a particular delivery date in mind?"

____

____

"Is there anything else you need before I total up this order?"

____

____

Let's jot down three sentences to encourage customers or prospective customers to do what you want them to do.

____

____

____

Monogram the Call

Most people have something monogrammed, such as a shirt, a pen, or maybe a ring. Monograms personalize an item. Names are a form of monogram. People like their names. They want them pronounced and spelled correctly.

When you know the customer's name, use it! When you know the party you are calling, or when callers tell you their name, use it immediately, and sprinkle it throughout the conversation. Everyone likes to hear their name—but be careful not to abuse it.

Example of name abuse:

> *"Hi, Mr. Jones. I wanted to tell you about our new financial planning software. Now, Mr. Jones, when you use it, you'll see a big improvement. And Mr. Jones, let me tell you the difference in graphics is very obvious. And one more thing Mr. Jones, we've got a special limited time offer. Mr. Jones? Mr. Jones? Hello?"*

MR. JONES starts thinking to himself: "I'm going to change my name."

A more effective method:

> *"Hi, Mr. Jones. Nice to meet you by phone. I want to tell you about our newest financial planning software product. You'll notice a difference in speed of data retrieval. And one more thing, Mr. Jones..."*

Using the name once or twice sounds nice, and it is effective. It shows you are paying attention. Use it too many times, and the effect is lost.

℞

1. When you know the other party's name use it in your conversation

2. Don't overdo it.

Monogram the Call

Telephone Doctor® says, "KNOW THE NAME? USE THE NAME!" Addressing your customer by name goes a long way toward overcoming the impersonal nature of a telephone contact. Why would it make such a difference?

_____

_____

As with most ideas, using the customer's name can backfire if it isn't done correctly. What are some of the mistakes you should avoid in this area?

_____

_____

For each of the situations below, write down an opening sentence that uses the other party's name. KNOW THE NAME? USE THE NAME!

1. You've just dialed the number of your customer contact at the Reely Grate Company. You found out last week that a new person has been assigned to the position, but you haven't spoken with the new buyer yet. The phone is answered and the person says, "Good morning, Purchasing Department, this is Hugh."

    _____

2. Your boss, Mrs. Sherman is attending a conference today and you've been asked to take a call for her. The caller on hold is Mr. Peabody, from the Wehback Machine Company.

    _____

3. Marian Church, who owns Church Wedding Services, has just opened an office in your area. She got your name from one of her clients and has called to inquire about setting up an account with your company. She's been on hold for about 30 seconds.

    _____

Naturally Inquisitive

There's a fine line between being naturally inquisitive and being nosy. Nosy questions ask for information that is NOYB–None of Your Business. When you're talking with a caller the following might be perceived as "nosy."

Example:

> "Hey, big guy. How much do you weigh?"

That question is nosy–and NOYB.

Example:

> "Tell me about your last W2. What did you end up pulling down last year?"

Way too nosy. And again, NOYB.

However, there are questions that are legitimate. Asking pertinent questions (questions that pertain to the conversation) is the key. Learn to be naturally inquisitive, instead of nosy, and you'll get better and more useful information.

It is easy to ask pertinent questions–you simply expand on what the caller is saying. By doing that, you're being naturally inquisitive, and you will obtain more information. That will often help you serve your customer better and build rapport.

Example:

Let's say you are talking to Mr. Jones and learn that he is a new employee with his company.

You:	(Being naturally inquisitive:) "And where were you before?"
Mr. Jones:	"I was in Dallas with Asset Dissipater."
You:	"Small world. I was just in Dallas last month, visiting some clients. Are you familiar with Gateway Controls?"
Mr. Jones:	"More than a small world...my wife worked there."

You got more information by being naturally inquisitive, by asking one *pertinent* question. Also, when you are naturally inquisitive and ask additional questions that pertain to the conversation, you show you are interested. In addition, you will become adept at communicating more clearly, uncovering your customer's needs, and building rapport and strong relationships.

NATURALLY INQUISITIVE

Asking nosy or irrelevant questions can cause serious problems in dealing with customers. However, not all personal questions are nosy. How can the right kind of personal question actually help customer service?

_____

_____

If asking the right kind of question is helpful and asking the wrong kind is harmful, it's essential to know the difference. What are the main characteristics of a naturally inquisitive question?

_____

_____

Which of these are naturally inquisitive rather than too nosy?

A.   We're building an addition to our house.
     1. I bet you're excited. When do they start?
     2. Wow! How much will that cost?

B.   It's my birthday.
     1. Well, happy birthday…enjoy…and many more.
     2. How old are you?

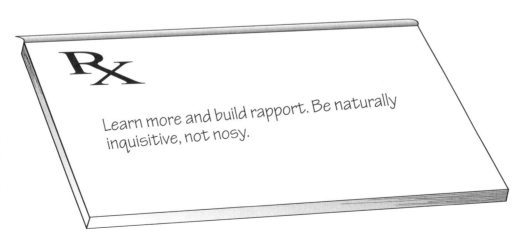

Learn more and build rapport. Be naturally inquisitive, not nosy.

Answers: A. 1, B. 2

One-Word Answers

"Yes."

"No."

"Okay."

"Fine."

What do you think when you get these answers? Most people will perceive one-word answers like these as being rude, cold, and uncaring.

Imagine you are at a party and you are introduced to an important guest. You talk to that person and all he gives you are one-word answers.

When you hear "Yep," "Nope," "Fine," and "Okay," immediately you sense that something is not right. You get the feeling that this person doesn't want to listen to you. One-word answers are unfriendly. When you use them, your callers are apt to think that perhaps you don't really want to help or talk to them. In reality, it takes only a few extra words to turn a one-word answer into a sentence.

Example:

Instead of saying "right," add a few words to make it:

> *"Yes, Mrs. Smith, that's exactly right."*

Instead of "Monday," try:

> *"Mrs. Smith, you can expect your delivery on Monday."*

Avoid one-word answers. There's no cost for the extra words. They're free. Use them!

ONE-WORD ANSWERS

At first, the use of one-word answers may seem like a good idea. The difficulty is that one-word answers may send unintended messages. What are some of these?

_____

_____

To keep from giving your customer the wrong impression, guard against using one-word answers. What specific techniques can you use to accomplish this?

_____

_____

Extra words are free, so be generous. Avoid one-word answers.

Practice Being Positive

"It's too hot."

"I'm too cold."

"I'm so tired."

"Thank goodness it's almost five o'clock."

Blah, blah, blah. No one wants to hear those complaints. If you have them, keep them to yourself. Try to maintain a positive attitude in both your professional and personal life.

If you are on the phone, you should practice the art of being positive with each and every caller. If customers hear negative comments about your company, product or service, they may think that there is more wrong with the company than you are telling them. It makes them wonder if they are doing business with the right people.

Sometimes a customer will make a comment, maybe just to make conversation, and he gets back a negative response.

> **Rep:** *"Hi, Mr. Johnson, it's Tom Lee at Acme Sales."*
>
> **Mr. Johnson:** *"Hi, Tom, how's it going today?"*
>
> **Rep:** *"Oh, not too bad for a Monday."*

What is Mr. Johnson supposed to think? Actually, anything he wants to. And it probably won't be good.

Here's another negative example:

> **Mr. Johnson:** *"Good afternoon, Joe, you doing okay today?"*
>
> **Rep:** *"I'll be doing a lot better in about an hour when I get out of here."*

Remember the caller doesn't need to know everything. If a customer asks, "How's business been?" and business has been slow, it is not your job to tell the caller this.

A good answer might be:

"We're doing just fine, Mr. Jones. How can I help you today?"

Mr. Negative might tell the caller:

"You're the first real prospect I've talked to today."

Again, what's Mr. Johnson to think? If no one else is doing business with Acme, should he? When someone asks a question just to make conversation, always try to give a positive response.

Example:

    Customer: *"Doing okay today?"*

        You: *"Sure am, how about you?"*

Your answers to such everyday questions can affect the customer's perception of your company, products, services, and you. Practice being positive!

If a customer question calls for a comment, make yours a positive one.

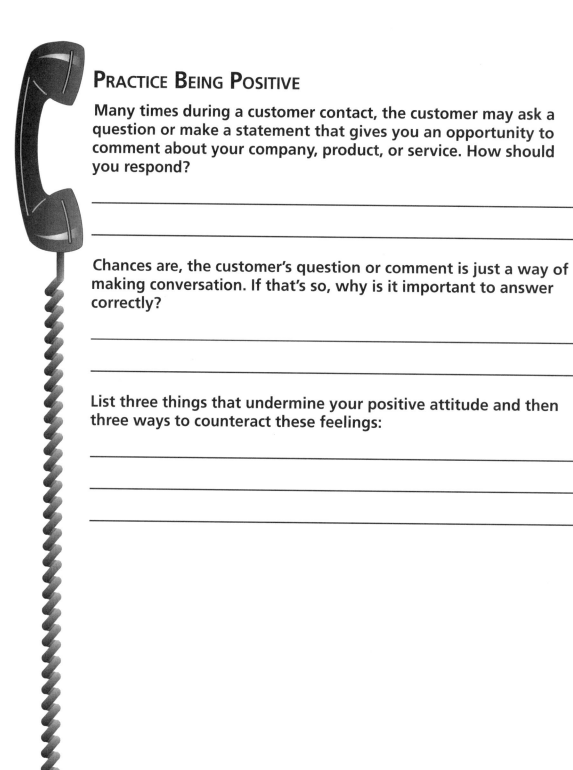

PRACTICE BEING POSITIVE

Many times during a customer contact, the customer may ask a question or make a statement that gives you an opportunity to comment about your company, product, or service. How should you respond?

_____

_____

Chances are, the customer's question or comment is just a way of making conversation. If that's so, why is it important to answer correctly?

_____

_____

List three things that undermine your positive attitude and then three ways to counteract these feelings:

_____

_____

_____

Qualifying

One of the most basic principles in selling on the phone or in person is to qualify—to sell to the person who can buy. It sounds simple, but it's not. Many employees are authorized to buy only a certain dollar amount, or they can only approve reorders of existing products.

There are lots of people who can say, "No," or "Okay, I'll tell the boss," but not many can say "Yes" all by themselves. Ideally, you want to talk to the decision maker, the person who can say "Yes."

How to Identify the Decision Maker

If you come right out and ask, "Do you have the authority to buy?" you'll probably offend someone. In fact, to keep from admitting that he has no power to purchase, sometimes the person will dodge the question rather than answer it. You might get the proverbial, "I want to think it over," while he goes to someone else for a decision. They don't want to "lose face." These people are commonly referred to as *the recommender*.

There are some very gentle ways to identify the decision maker without offending the person you're talking with:

➤ *Expect* that someone else is involved in the decision making.

➤ Try to have the person you're talking with come right out and tell you, "Yes I can," or "No, I need to check with someone else for a decision on an approval."

To accomplish this, ask questions like:

> *"Let's say you like the program, Mr. Jones, What needs to happen for us to do business? Who else is involved in the ordering process?"*

> *"If you want to go ahead with this, who else do we need to include and impress to get going?"*

> *"Most of my clients have several people involved in a purchasing decision. Who else at your company is included in the process?"*

By *expecting* others to be involved, you are making it easy and natural for your prospects to tell you it is their decision, or to give you the names of the other key players. Again, this allows the person you are calling to save face.

If you go ahead with a presentation and assume the person you're talking with is the decision maker, several things can happen:

1. You can make a perfectly marvelous presentation, use all your energy and all your good material, and come up empty—all because the person you're talking with isn't able to buy. Learn to qualify ahead of time and be sure you're talking with the person who can buy.

2. If an unqualified customer tells you they'll pass along your information, don't count on the sale. They'll neither remember one-half of what you said, nor will they tell it with the same enthusiasm, knowledge, and conviction that you can. I don't think any actor on Broadway doing a show would let you or me stand in for him. That's what you're doing if you let someone else tell your story—you're letting an amateur do the work of a professional.

3. It is simply not good salesmanship to let someone else do the work. When a decision is being made and you're absent from the scene, a successful outcome is in doubt.

Rx

When qualifying a prospect, presume someone else is involved.

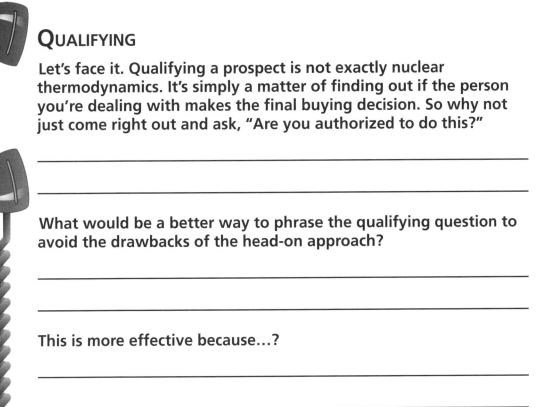

QUALIFYING

Let's face it. Qualifying a prospect is not exactly nuclear thermodynamics. It's simply a matter of finding out if the person you're dealing with makes the final buying decision. So why not just come right out and ask, "Are you authorized to do this?"

_____

_____

What would be a better way to phrase the qualifying question to avoid the drawbacks of the head-on approach?

_____

_____

This is more effective because...?

_____

_____

Rejection

From time to time, everyone in a sales position experiences rejection. Some general rejection statements are usually close to these:

> *"No, I don't want any."*
>
> *"Cancel my order."*
>
> *"I already bought from your competition."*
>
> *"I'm not interested."*

These are just some examples of the rejection salespeople experience. The important part is how you handle the rejection. Somewhere between not caring at all to being personally crushed is where you need to be. No one enjoys rejection. Unfortunately it comes with most sales jobs. The important thing is not to take it personally.

When you get a rejection, the customer is usually rejecting one of these factors:

1. The offer

2. The company

3. The product

4. The price

5. The timing

6. Some other outside factor

There are six items on that list. Notice that *not one of them is you.*

REJECTION

It's never pleasant to be rejected, especially when putting forth your time and effort to make the sale. How do you keep from taking these rejections personally?

_____

_____

When I need to reject others, I try to do it gently. Some of the words and phrases I use when rejecting others are:

_____

_____

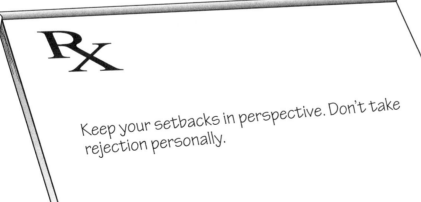

Keep your setbacks in perspective. Don't take rejection personally.

STU 8 Smile

A Telephone Doctor® book would not be complete without the mention of a smile. Like sunshine warms up a summer day, a smile warms up your conversation. It is an expression of friendliness.

And yes, you can *hear* a smile! Tests have proven this over and over again. When you are smiling, your enthusiasm comes through the telephone, and it's recognized by your caller.

A thought about voicemail: Surveys show that a smiling message will be responded to more often than a dull, uninteresting one.

How can you remember to keep smiling? Here's a Telephone Doctor® tip. Keep a mirror by your phone where you can see your facial expression as you're talking. It works!

FACT: It takes more muscles to frown than it does to smile. (So why overwork?)

℞

1. SMILE! Your customers can hear it!

2. Keep a mirror by your phone to check your facial expressions as you talk.

Sᴍɪʟᴇ

Whether you're talking with a customer in person or on the phone, it's important to remember to smile. Why?

_____

_____

If the person on the other end of the line can't see you, what difference does it make if you're smiling or not?

_____

_____

Ask a friend to leave you a two-sentence message on your voicemail or answering machine. Tell him or her to leave identical messages, but only smile while they are leaving one of them. When you listen to the messages, you will definitely hear the difference.

STU 8

Tone of Voice

True Tales

Several years ago, I interviewed a young lady for a phone position. She was bright, friendly, fun, and positive. We talked for quite a while, and because of her enthusiasm, I hired her on the spot. After a few weeks of training, she went on the phones calling Telephone Doctor® clients.

I happened to walk past her office one day shortly after she got on the phones and I nearly fell over. It looked like the same person, but it didn't sound like the same person. She was dull, unfriendly, cold, and impersonal.

I called her into my office. "What happened to the tone of voice and enthusiasm I heard in the interview?" I asked. "You were wonderful!"

She said, "Oh, that was for you. I use a different tone when I'm on a business call."

"Wrong," I told her. "Business callers deserve a bright, friendly tone of voice too."

There is a big difference between a bright cheery voice and a dull tone of voice, even when you use the same words. A good tone of voice is so important on the phone. It sets the entire mood of the relationship. Callers tend to mirror your tone. When you are upbeat and bright, chances are they will be too! Truly, it is often not *what* you say, but *how* you say it!

P.S. Guess who doesn't work at Telephone Doctor® anymore!

R̞x

Use a warm, friendly tone with your customers. They deserve it.

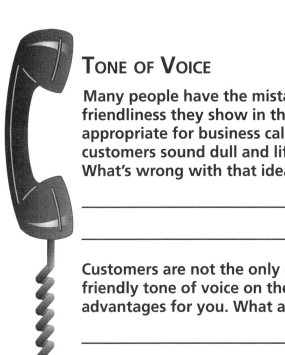

TONE OF VOICE

Many people have the mistaken idea that the warmth and friendliness they show in their personal conversations is not appropriate for business calls. As a result, their conversations with customers sound dull and lifeless, if not downright unfriendly. What's wrong with that idea?

_____

_____

Customers are not the only ones to benefit from your use of a friendly tone of voice on the telephone. There are also definite advantages for you. What are some of them?

_____

_____

To better understand the impact of tone of voice, say these three sentences in the various tones and check them off as you do so.

1. I love my job.

❏ Happy   ❏ Angry   ❏ Sad   ❏ Sincere   ❏ Non-committal

2. You did what?

❏ Happy   ❏ Angry   ❏ Sad   ❏ Sincere   ❏ Non-committal

3. Thank you so very much.

❏ Happy   ❏ Angry   ❏ Sad   ❏ Sincere   ❏ Non-committal

STU 8 Understanding Needs

When you stop to think about it, needs are the root of all sales situations, aren't they? A sale can only take place if a customer has a need and you are able to *identify* and *fulfill* that need with your product or service. Some needs are actually a combination of many needs. This may sound simple, but it is a very important concept to understand.

Your customer may be needing:

➤ Higher quality

➤ Faster delivery

➤ Greater savings

➤ Improved safety

➤ Better service

➤ Higher performance

➤ Increased productivity

Whatever the need is, it is critically important to you to both uncover it and understand it. Develop a list of simple statements to help you in this process.

Example:

> *"Mrs. Evans, if you were going to try out a new bank, what do you think your biggest reason for doing so would be?"*

Another great way to "uncover" a client need:

> *"Mr. Kelly, what would you rate as the most critical element in your decision to upgrade your policy?"*

These types of questions can help determine the need or needs of your customers and facilitate the sales of your product or service.

Taking the time to stop and ask questions is key. Customers sometimes think they know what they need when actually, after a short discussion, you can know more about what they need than they do.

Tell customers that in order for you to meet their needs it is important you ask some questions. That way, the questions aren't a surprise, and, in general, will be accepted.

You will have a much better chance of selling to customers when you understand their needs. Take the time to find out what they are. Notice that most of the "understanding needs" questions start with a "W" such as Who, What, Where, Why, and When. These are great words for uncovering needs—and understanding them.

Customer needs are critically important. Uncover and understand them.

UNDERSTANDING NEEDS

Most people agree that one of the most important elements in excellent customer service is exceeding customer need. But we can't meet what we don't know, and the customer needs are not always obvious from the start, especially when we initiate the contact. How do we determine these needs?

_____

_____

Good listening skills are important in any customer contact, but especially so in understanding customer needs. Why?

_____

_____

List three ways to ask your customers questions that will uncover their specific needs so that you understand them.

1. _____

2. _____

3. _____

Vary Your Responses

There is a wonderful old saying, "If you always do what you've always done, you'll always get what you always got."

Many of us tend to do the same thing over and over again. We go to the same restaurants, hang out with the same people, drive the same type of automobile, and so on. It's not a rut, it's just that people get used to things being a certain way. It makes us feel comfortable. Yet at times it is important that we move out of our "comfort zone."

This happens very easily with words. People tend to attach themselves to certain phrases and use them over and over again. Are you a victim of this habit?

Example:

> **Caller:** *"Can you help me? There's a problem with a check in my checking account. My name is Betty Ross."*
>
> **You:** *"Okay."*
>
> **Caller:** *"Here's my account number: 11-43-77-46-2."*
>
> **You:** *"Okay."*
>
> **Caller:** *"I show check #1230 for $250. You have it on my statement for $280."*
>
> **You:** *"Okay."*

"Okay, okay, okay!" That's easy enough to fix. There are so many other confirming phrases that can be used.

Example:

Caller:	*"Can you help me? There's a problem with one check in my checking account. My name is Betty Ross."*
You:	*"I'll be glad to help, Ms. Ross. And the number of the check is...?"*
Caller:	*"I show check #1230 for $250. You have it on my statement for $280."*
You:	*"Let's see what I can find out for you."*

Show some personality! Remember to vary your responses so the caller isn't hearing the same word over and over again. Okay, okay, okay?

R̴x

1. Vary your responses.

2. Have a list of different responses in front of you as you talk.

VARY YOUR RESPONSES

We all have certain words, phrases, or expressions that we use often. We need to be careful not to overuse these in dealing with our customers. What wrong messages could we be sending by using the same responses over and over?

1. _____

2. _____

3. _____

What can you do to avoid "getting into a rut" with your same responses?

_____

_____

List as many confirmation words and phrases as you can (we've started the list for you).

1. Right

2. Good

3. OK

4. Very well

5.

6.

7.

8.

9.

10.

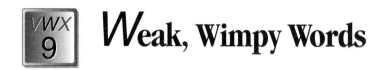

Weak, Wimpy Words

What are weak, wimpy words? Which of the following sound stronger?

"I think you'll like this brochure."

or,

"You're really going to like this brochure."

Here's another one:

"I think we can have the policy issued by Tuesday."

or,

"You will have the policy by Tuesday."

Remove the word *think* from your sentence when you need to sound more confident.

Naturally, there are places where the word *think* may be appropriate, like when you are actually thinking about something. But don't use *I think* to mean "I'm not sure." In most cases, you'll strengthen the statement when you eliminate the word *think*.

Another weak, wimpy word that most sentences can do well without is *just*. It is as though you're humbly asking permission.

Example:

"Hi, I'm just calling to hear what you thought of the idea we talked about."

Listen to how much more confident this sounds:

"Hi, I'm calling to hear what you thought of the idea we talked about."

Eliminate the words *think* and *just*. Two other weak, wimpy words are *possibly* and *maybe*. Remove these and all other weak, wimpy words and you will become far more effective. You will be making confident statements rather than ones of doubt!

WEAK, WIMPY WORDS

You may never have considered that words can be strong or weak. But the fact is that certain words like "think" and "just" are often used in ways that make them weak and wimpy. Why is that important to you in communicating effectively with customers?

_____

_____

Avoiding weak words in your customer contacts means changing old habits. How can you be sure you're on track?

_____

_____

List some of your own weak, wimpy words:

-              •
-              •
-              •
-              •

Share your confidence with your customer.
Avoid weak, wimpy words.

X-Out Credibility Busters

Are you a credible salesperson? You might not be aware of it, but there are certain phrases you use which, unfortunately, can act as "credibility busters." Taken at face value these phrases sound as though you are actually trying to *add* credibility.

Example:

> *"Let me be honest with you."*

or,

> *"To tell you the truth..."*

When a prospect or business associate hears these, it may make them wonder if you were truthful before you made the proclamation.

Example:

> **Caller:** *"Are you sure this is the best plan for my budget?"*
>
> **You:** *"Well, can I be honest with you?"*
>
> **Caller:** *"No, actually I was hoping you'd lie to me."*

Here are a few other credibility busters:

> *"Let me be perfectly frank."*

or,

> *"Can I level with you?"*

Your callers expect you to be frank and honest with them, and to tell them the truth. Eliminate credibility busters!

X-Out Credibility Busters

In an effort to add emphasis or establish rapport with a customer, some people use expressions like "to tell you the truth..." or "let me be honest with you." Why are phrases like these referred to as "credibility busters"?

_____

_____

Avoiding these credibility busting phrases doesn't mean you can't verbally highlight the key parts of your conversation with customers. It's simply a matter of finding replacements for these expressions. What alternatives can you think of?

_____

_____

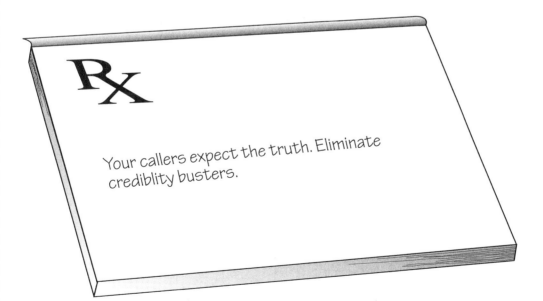

Rx

Your callers expect the truth. Eliminate crediblity busters.

Yes

"Yes, I'd like to order the magazine."

"Yes, you can count me in."

"Yes, I have the money."

"Yes, here's your order."

Yes, yes, yes. To a salesperson, the most beautiful word in the English language is often *yes*.

In sales, you know that it takes a lot of *no's* to get to that one *yes*. And when you do, there is a certain kind of high–a feeling that cannot be described.

In order to get a *yes* in sales, you need to use all your talents and personality. It is not just one thing that gets an order, it is a combination platter. It could be your tone of voice, your understanding of the customer's needs, or a benefit you shared. And yes, it could be the smile in your voice. It could be anything from A to Z. Whatever it is, getting the customer to agree with you, and telling you yes is your ultimate goal.

YES

Yes is a small, yet powerful and exciting word in sales. List some other words that the customer can say to let you know they'll "go ahead" with what you're offering.

_____

_____

Make a list of questions that will get you the YES answer you want from your customers. Use them.

-
-
-
-
-
-

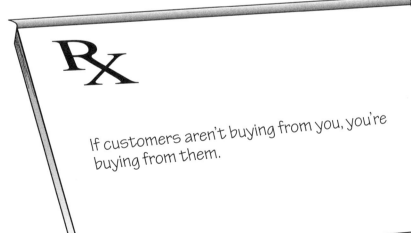

If customers aren't buying from you, you're buying from them.

Be Creative

Zeal... Zest... Zipper... Zero... this is the last letter of the alphabet for telemarketing skills.

Now, it is no secret that "Z" is a tough letter when you are writing an A to Z book.

The next time you run into a tough situation while you're on the phone, remember to be creative. Use your imagination to solve the problem. It doesn't always need to make perfect sense. Think outside of the box!

Z-End

As you carry on with your daily routine, you probably find that there are certain problems or situations that occur repeatedly. You may even have wished there were better ways to approach or solve these. Unfortunately, wishing doesn't accomplish much. What can you do?

_____

_____

What if it doesn't work?

_____

_____

Z - END!

Test Your Telemarketing Savvy

Once you have completed this book, take a few minutes to complete this quiz as a review of what you've learned.

1. To help you deal with the stresses you encounter every day, it's important to remember that the one thing you always control is:
   a. your environment.
   b. your attitude.
   c. your workload.

2. When a customer makes a negative comment, asking for details just makes things worse.
   ❑ T ❑ F

3. Which of the following is NOT one of the main details that should be included with each telephone message you take?
   a. the caller's name
   b. the caller's telephone number
   c. the caller's social security number

4. Which of the following is the best closing word or phrase?
   a. Why don't you just...
   b. Let's...
   c. All you have to do is...

5. Monogramming the call means:
   a. using the customer's name whenever possible.
   b. identifying yourself to the customer only by your initials.
   c. using the customer's name at least twice during the call.

6. If things are slow, or you're having a bad day, that should never be communicated to your customers.

   ❏ T   ❏ F

7. You can best communicate warmth and friendlessness to customers on the phone by:

   a. tone of your voice.

   b. smiling before you pick up the phone.

   c. both a and b are recommended.

8. The only difference between nosy and naturally inquisitive is the way you ask the question.

   ❏ T   ❏ F

9. Words like "maybe" and "possibly"

   a. show your cooperative spirit with customers.

   b. are weak and wimpy and should be avoided.

   c. give your customers confidence in you.

10. Sometimes the most effective way to determine customers' needs is to have them tell you.

    ❏ T   ❏ F

Answers: 1. B, 2. F, 3. C, 4. B, 5. A, 6. T, 7. C, 8. T, 9. B, 10. T.

Additional Reading

Finch, Lloyd. *Call Center Success*. Menlo Park, CA: Crisp Publications, 2000.

Finch, Lloyd. *Success as a CSR*. Menlo Park, CA: Crisp Publications, 1998.

Finch, Lloyd and Vivyan Finch. *Telemarketing*. Menlo Park, CA: Crisp Publications, 1995.

Finch, Lloyd. *Telephone Courtesy & Customer Service*. Menlo Park, CA: Crisp Publications, 2000.

Finch, Lloyd. *Twenty Ways to Improve Customer Service*. Menlo Park, CA: Crisp Publications, 1994.

Freestone, Julie. *Telemarketing Basics*. Menlo Park, CA: Crisp Publications, 1989.

Friedman, Nancy. *Customer Service Nightmares*. Menlo Park, CA: Crisp Publications, 2000.

Friedman, Nancy. *Telephone Skills from A to Z*. Menlo Park, CA: Crisp Publications, 2000.

Gerson, Richard. *Winning at the Inner Game of Selling*, Menlo Park, CA: Crisp Publications, 1999.

Martin, William. *Quality Customer Service*. Menlo Park, CA: Crisp Publications, 2001.

Parker, Emily. *Closing Sales & Winning Your Customer's Heart*. Menlo Park, CA: Crisp Publications, 2000.

Thornton, Virden. *Building & Closing the Sale*. Menlo Park, CA: Crisp Publications, 2001.

Now Available From

Books•Videos•CD-ROMs•Computer-Based Training Products

Subject Areas Include:

Management
Human Resources
Communication Skills
Personal Development
Marketing/Sales
Organizational Development
Customer Service/Quality
Computer Skills
Small Business and Entrepreneurship
Adult Literacy and Learning
Life Planning and Retirement

CRISP WORLDWIDE DISTRIBUTION

English language books are distributed worldwide. Major international distributors include:

ASIA/PACIFIC

Australia/New Zealand: In Learning, PO Box 1051, Springwood QLD, Brisbane, Australia 4127   Tel: 61-7-3-841-2286, Facsimile: 61-7-3-841-2618
ATTN: Messrs. Gordon

Philippines: National Book Store Inc., Quad Alpha Centrum Bldg, 125 Pioneer Street, Mandaluyong, Metro Manila, Philippines   Tel: 632-631-8051, Facsimile: 632-631-5016

Singapore, Malaysia, Brunei, Indonesia: Times Book Shops. Direct sales HQ:
STP Distributors, Pasir Panjang Distrientre, Block 1 #03-01A, Pasir Panjang Rd, Singapore 118480   Tel: 65-2767626, Facsimile: 65-2767119

Japan: Phoenix Associates Co., Ltd., Mizuho Bldng, 3-F, 2-12-2, Kami Osaki, Shinagawa-Ku, Tokyo 141   Tel: 81-33-443-7231, Facsimile: 81-33-443-7640
ATTN: Mr. Peter Owans

CANADA

Crisp Learning Canada, 60 Briarwood Avenue, Mississauga, ON L5G 3N6 Canada
Tel: (905) 274-5678, Facsimile: (905) 278-2801
ATTN: Mr. Steve Connolly/Mr. Jerry McNabb

Trade Book Stores: Raincoast Books, 8680 Cambie Street,
Vancouver, BC V6P 6M9 Canada
Tel: (604) 323-7100, Facsimile: (604) 323-2600   ATTN: Order Desk

EUROPEAN UNION

England: Flex Training, Ltd., 9-15 Hitchin Street,
Baldock, Hertfordshire, SG7 6A, England
Tel: 44-1-46-289-6000, Facsimile: 44-1-46-289-2417   ATTN: Mr. David Willetts

INDIA

Multi-Media HRD, Pvt., Ltd., National House,
Tulloch Road, Appolo Bunder, Bombay, India 400-039
Tel: 91-22-204-2281, Facsimile: 91-22-283-6478   ATTN: Messrs. Aggarwal

SOUTH AMERICA

Mexico: Grupo Editorial Iberoamerica, Nebraska 199, Col. Napoles, 03810 Mexico, D.F.
Tel: 525-523-0994, Facsimile: 525-543-1173   ATTN: Señor Nicholas Grepe

SOUTH AFRICA

Alternative Books, PO Box 1345, Ferndale 2160, South Africa
Tel: 27-11-792-7730, Facsimile: 27-11-792-7787   ATTN: Mr. Vernon de Haas

VER.E